SHORT AND SWEET

Quick Creative Writing Activities that Encourage Imagination, Humor and Enthusiasm for Writing

Randy Larson

Illustrated by Patricia Howard

Cottonwood Press, Inc.
Fort Collins, Colorado

Requests for permission should be addressed to:

Cottonwood Press, Inc.
109-B Cameron Drive
Fort Collins, Colorado 80525

Web: www.cottonwoodpress.com
Email: cottonwood@cottonwoodpress.com
Phone: 1-800-864-4297
Fax: 970-204-0761

ISBN 1-877673-19-6

This book is dedicated to Anne Charter,
my high school English teacher at Gwinn High School.
She pointed the way.

Table of Contents

Introduction

Short and Sweet was written with the intention of getting kids to say, "Hey, this is cool. Let me borrow a pen, okay?" The exercises in the book are designed to stir students' imaginations, to create an immediate interest in writing, and to provide exercises brief enough that all students, regardless of ability or skill level, can complete them.

Short. The word "Short" in the title means just that. The exercises are designed to be completed quickly, in less than a class period. Teachers who need a warmer-upper on a flat Monday morning, or a finisher-offer on a wild Friday afternoon, can get quick results with *Short and Sweet.* A substitute teacher with shaky or non-existent plans can get things rolling with a quick ten or fifteen-minute *Short and Sweet* writing exercise. When a new teacher finds that the lesson on topic sentences has ended 20 minutes too soon, he or she can say, "Okay, here's a *Short and Sweet* exercise for today. I'll be coming around the room looking for a solid topic sentence in your writing, and I'll be sure to save time for some of you to share what you have written." That is an important part of *Short and Sweet* — sharing. Students will enjoy writing on the unusual topics, knowing that they will have an audience to appreciate what they have created.

Sweet. The word "Sweet" in the title means that the writing assignments are palatable enough to make students want to come back to the writing process, again and again. Gifted students and high-risk students alike will enjoy offbeat writing activities like writing parodies of tabloid-style newspapers, telling about the unluckiest person in the world appearing on a game show, making up dramatic stories to explain a cast or bandage, or concocting Rare Vegetables Federation rescues for endangered pumpkins. Writing activities like these get the attention of today's young people and keep them on task.

Uses. *Short and Sweet* can be used as a class reward, as a learning check ("I'll be looking for one sentence with commas in a series," or "Show me a compound sentence in your work."), as a motivator for a lackluster group of non-writers who had no choice but to take your class, as a filler on days when the glass-blowing acrobat arrived an hour late for the morning assembly, or as a simple way for teachers to get closer to their students by laughing with them, commenting on their work, complimenting valiant efforts and appreciating creative bursts that will surely come from students who may never before have seemed capable of a fresh thought or an unusual perspective.

Have fun with your students as they have fun with *Short and Sweet.*

Randy Larson

Endangered Pumpkins

You are the new director of the Rare Vegetables Federation. You have received a report that the Siberian Exploding Pumpkin is in trouble. It is a rare species of pumpkin that grows on the Siberian plains in the dead of winter and reseeds itself by exploding during the first full moon in spring.

There are five of these pumpkins left in the world, but they have been hijacked and stashed in a garage in Sausalito, California. A woman known in the seed business as Hybrid Hazel is holding the pumpkins ransom to the highest bidder. Her estate is protected by both guard dogs and a laser beam pumpkin protection system. Getting the rare Siberian Pumpkins back will not be easy.

You must write up a plan to rescue the Siberian Exploding Pumpkins from the hands of Hazel and her horrible helpers. It will be a dangerous mission, perhaps similar to the time the Rare Vegetables Federation's Cucumber Commandos raided a French seed company and stole back two dozen long-stemmed cucumbers lifted from the Museum of Classical Vegetables in Paris.

Your plan must be shrewd. It must be properly punctuated. And it must convince your members to once again risk their lives for an important vegetable. Write out your plan below. Good luck, and good writing!

_____

_____

_____

_____

_____

_____

_____

_____

_____

_____

_____

_____

_____

_____

_____

Darby and Donna Dooright

Darby and Donna Dooright are compulsive "do-gooders." They are determined to spread joy and good cheer throughout the world by any means possible. They put nickels in the change return slot of pay phones so that people who check for coins will find a small surprise. They let people go ahead of them in long lines at the movies, sweep the streets for free after parades and always leave the unused portion of their detergent at the laundromat.

Why do the Doorights do this? What else have they done? What will they do next? You, as a reporter for the *Foghorn Gazette*, have been assigned to do a feature story on Darby and Donna Dooright. Follow them for a week and write your account of their generous but unusual behavior.

_____

_____

_____

_____

_____

_____

_____

_____

_____

_____

_____

_____

_____

_____

_____

_____

_____

Waxing Hysterical

Your class is on a field trip to a wax museum in the city. Everybody files into the museum and immediately scatters from one end of the building to the other. You find some interesting pamphlets about the characters on "Murderers' Row," a section of the museum that contains wax figures representing killers executed for their crimes.

You sit in a soft chair behind a stack of magazines to read the pamphlets for just a moment, but soon you fall fast asleep. Hours pass, and suddenly you are awake. It is dark, except for the lights at the base of the wax figures, lights that are throwing a weak, eerie glow into the room. You go to the door of "Murderers' Row" and turn the knob. It is bolted. There are no windows. You are trapped and alone. Suddenly a voice . . .

Finish the story.

_____

_____

_____

_____

_____

_____

_____

_____

_____

_____

_____

_____

_____

_____

_____

_____

_____

_____

_____

Testing, Testing

You are a student of psychology at Thinkum University, studying under Dr. Schlepp, a strange but famous psychologist with the weirdest theories ever developed about human behavior. Dr. Schlepp believes, for example, that people who bite off spaghetti noodles rather than sucking them in are afraid of the dark and also cannot be trusted with expensive cameras. He thinks that people who write with black ink have a tendency to marry red-haired dentists. He believes that people who won't ride Ferris wheels are always late for funerals.

You have been asked to complete a final exam in Dr. Schlepp's class. Your assignment is to write seven of *your* theories about human behavior. Good luck. (Feel free to be funny, but be kind. Don't write any "theories" that degrade a person or a group of people.)

_____

_____

_____

_____

_____

_____

_____

_____

_____

_____

_____

_____

_____

_____

_____

_____

_____

It All Started Like This

Some young people insist they have no creative juices whatsoever. Then they come up with the most long-winded, bizarre explanations for things that have gone wrong — things that they were involved in. For example, one of them might be attempting to make a strawberry malt in the family blender when the potion suddenly erupts and splatters the kitchen with pink goo. The parents walk in, and they hear, "Gee, you wouldn't believe what happened. It all started like this . . ." Then the young person goes into a long explanation that involves meteor showers, power surges, inconsiderate behavior on the part of little brothers, and the high price of gasoline in Europe.

Imagine yourself in each of the situations described below. Then make up a story that attempts to get you off the hook. Begin each "explanation" with these words: "It all started like this . . ."

1. Your parents discover that the family station wagon has a small, round hole in the windshield, and it wasn't there before.

2. Your mom turns on her computer and finds that the only thing left on the hard drive is a game called "Monster Mash."

3. Your parents find your report card under the toaster. There is a *D-* next to the word *science.*

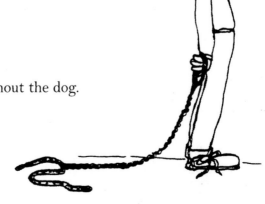

4. You come home without your $100.00 gym shoes.

5. You come home from walking the dog, without the dog.

A Pain in the Neck

Every once in a while someone will come to school or to work wearing a cast, a bandage or both. Everyone asks, "What happened?" For the next ten minutes the poor victim has to relive the horrors of the accident and the pain of the cure.

But it doesn't stop there. Next, someone will say, "That happened to me last year, but I broke my entire face." This person's story will be far worse than the first person's and will take much more time. Then another person will tell how she was at the zoo and was trampled by a herd of armadillos and had to have 452 stitches — but she's fine now. She will describe each of the armadillos and every doctor, nurse and attendant at the hospital. And on and on it goes.

Because most real-life accidents aren't all that dramatic, many of us don't have an awful cast or bandage story to tell. Maybe we tripped on the rug, fell taking out the trash, or bumped into an open drawer — boring. Now is the time to create something interesting. Make up a great cast or a bandage story that will top anything else you have ever heard.

_____

_____

_____

_____

_____

_____

_____

_____

_____

_____

_____

_____

_____

_____

_____

Moonwalk

Imagine the eerie feeling of standing on the dry, dead surface of the moon, staring back at the earth that is floating free in the blackness of space. Are you thinking of the vast distance of 240,000 miles between you and homework? Are you thinking about how there is no "road" back? Can you spot your native country beneath the white, swirling clouds? Do you want to return, or do you want to go out even farther into space? Are you afraid, worried, excited, hopeful, depressed, calm, assured, happy?

Write your thoughts and feelings as you stand on the moon looking back at the place that gave you birth and life.

_____

_____

_____

_____

_____

_____

_____

_____

_____

_____

_____

_____

_____

_____

Mail-Order Heart Throb

Years ago people could order houses out of the Sears catalog. They also ordered complete automobiles, farm buildings, farm machinery, and just about anything else needed for life — except husbands and wives.

What if you *could* use a catalog to order a spouse, or even a boyfriend or girlfriend? Can you picture such a publication? How would it be written? How would the "products" be presented?

On the lines below, write out an ad for the boyfriend or girlfriend *you* would like to order, the person of your dreams. Describe his or her physical appearance, attitudes, feelings, perspectives on life and love, family background, future plans, hopes, dreams, fears — anything that might be appropriate.

_____

_____

_____

_____

_____

_____

_____

_____

_____

_____

_____

_____

_____

_____

_____

_____

_____

_____

Practically Joking

There once was a lady with a neighbor who constantly boasted about the mileage he got from his new compact car. Every time he saw the woman out in her yard pruning roses or training her cocker spaniel, he would lean over the fence and say something like, "That little car. What a dandy. Got 49 miles per gallon last week. Can't believe it!"

After six months of mileage reports, the woman decided to teach her neighbor a lesson. Every night for a month she sneaked over to the man's house and poured a gallon of gasoline into his tank. His gas mileage became more and more fantastic. "I'm up to 145 miles per gallon!" he said one Saturday morning. "Can you believe it? No one's got a car like this, I'll bet. I'm going to call CNN. I think I've got a story here." And so he did. The news people came and took his car and tested it, and you know, of course, what they found. The woman tended her roses in peace after that. The neighbor went out and bought a truck.

Imagine a great practical joke of your own, and describe it. Be specific. Be clever. Have fun!

_____

_____

_____

_____

_____

_____

_____

_____

_____

_____

_____

_____

_____

_____

_____

_____

_____

_____

1-900-PIMPLES

You are the person with a new, homemade cure for pimples. Everyone around you is begging for the recipe, but you won't tell.

Your inspiration came one day while reading the new book, *Squeeze 'Em and Weep*, by Mavis Takayuramota, Ph.D. From her suggestions and 12 common household products, you devised a concoction that makes bumpy pimples disappear.

Now you have set up a 1-900-PIMPLES phone line that costs $15 per minute for teens in trouble. They get to listen to your expert pimple advice. You sympathize with your callers because you remember the pain of walking into a room with a shopping bag over your head.

You are in your office waiting for that first call from a serious pimple victim. There it is! The phone is ringing! Reach out and heal someone! What are you going to say?

_____

_____

_____

_____

_____

_____

_____

_____

_____

_____

_____

_____

_____

_____

_____

_____

_____

_____

_____

_____

Widgets for Sale

There are companies all over the United States that sell things that might be called wacky widgets. Wacky widgets are silly, strange and for the most part, useless. But people buy them anyway, for gag gifts, office parties and practical jokes.

One company sells fake bloody arms that you can hang out your car window or stuff under your door. Others make lifelike legs, giant rubber cockroaches, pop cans that snore, exploding golf balls, electric massage shoes or barking dog bones.

What if a company came out with a catalog of wacky widgets just for students and teachers? What would these products look like? What would they do? Make up a title for such a catalog, and invent six products that you think are crazy enough to include. Describe the items with such detail that few people could resist ordering at least one.

_____

_____

_____

_____

_____

_____

_____

_____

_____

_____

_____

_____

_____

_____

_____

_____

_____

_____

_____

_____

_____

A Friendly Chat

You are on a park bench, and it is spring. People are walking, jogging, playing tennis, roller skating, biking and feeding the ducks on the pond. Suddenly, an elderly person steps up and asks, "May I sit here?"

You say, "Yes, of course," and the person sits down to watch the passersby.

As you look at the person out of the corner of your eye, a strange sensation comes over you. You notice the person's eyes, mouth, chin, the slope of the forehead, the angle of the nose. Then you look at the person's hands, and you see that the left one has a scar across the middle knuckle, just like yours.

A chill goes down your spine as you realize you are sitting next to yourself, 50 years into the future. Once the shock subsides, you decide to ask some questions of this "stranger." Write your conversation with this person who is the future you. Write your questions in such a way that the "stranger" never does find out who you really are.

_____

_____

_____

_____

_____

_____

_____

_____

_____

_____

_____

_____

_____

_____

_____

_____

_____

_____

Missing

It is Saturday morning and you wake up to silence — which isn't right. There is no riding lawn mower roaring outside your window. No traffic. No radio blaring from your sister's room. Just silence. You sit up in bed to find a room you don't recognize. There is a knock on the door. In comes a butler, holding a silver tray with breakfast goodies. You slam the door behind him and run to the mirror. There, staring back at you is the image of someone you recognize, someone famous — but certainly not you.

Who is it? Jennifer Lopez? Johnny Depp? Jackie Chan? Natalie Portman? LeBron James? Sammy Sosa? Someone else?

Whoever you are, pretend that you have a day to yourself, a day without crowds, business agents, coaches, fans or photographers surrounding you. What will you do? Where will you go? Will you take someone with you? How long will you be gone? Are you coming back? How will you conceal your identity while out in public? What will your mother say? Will this day make you happy? Will it make you a better person? Would you like another day like this one? Why? Why not?

_____

_____

_____

_____

_____

_____

_____

_____

_____

_____

_____

_____

_____

_____

Are We Having Fun Yet?

The "Vacation" films made years ago, starring Chevy Chase, were well attended by movie-goers. The films were popular partly because they had kernels of truth scattered throughout the ridiculous scenes that kept people laughing until they cried. Almost everyone can sympathize with two teenagers stuck in the back seat of a station wagon with an ancient aunt or uncle. And most of us know people who go overboard decorating their houses, yards and larger family possessions with holiday lights.

In your own words, describe what you would consider a "nightmare vacation." Tell what would be the worst place to visit, the worst people to travel with, the worst hotel you could imagine staying in, and the worst tourist attractions you could possibly see. Imagine the kinds of things that might go wrong, and describe all the misery you might encounter in your nightmare vacation.

_____

_____

_____

_____

_____

_____

_____

_____

_____

_____

_____

_____

_____

_____

_____

_____

_____

_____

Name _____

Pop Goes the Genie

It is Friday the 13th, and you are home alone while your parents are out with the Hendersons. The wind has picked up and is thrashing the lilac bushes against the house. The moon is throwing wild shadows across the window. Luckily, your dog Kibbles is in the entrance way, guarding the door, and your cat Snoozer, who has terrific hearing, is perched on the window seat.

Suddenly the doorbell rings and you jump from your chair. Kibbles howls and Snoozer leaps to the floor and arches her back, staring toward the kitchen. No one is supposed to drop by. All of your friends are at the Heavy Mushrooms concert, and you didn't order a pizza. Who could it be?

You approach the door cautiously and look through the peep hole. Nothing. The sidewalk is empty. The street is quiet. Nothing is moving, so you open the door an inch or so to get a better look. There on the bottom step sits a soft drink can that appears to be empty. But how could it stay there in the wind if nothing is in it? There is no one around, so you quickly grab the can and shut the door.

It is a soft drink brand you have never seen before, and the can looks as if it spent the night in the gutter. You grab a towel and begin to rub the dirt off the name. Suddenly, a puff of blue smoke shoots from the can, and a small fat genie in red boxer shorts and sunglasses appears. He says, "I'm Charlie Fizzle, the genie with sizzle! What can I do for you, kid?"

Finish the story. Tell about the strangest night of your life. Let your wishes run wild.

_____

_____

_____

_____

_____

_____

_____

_____

_____

Treasure at Midnight

Your parents have insisted that the whole family spend a day at the waterfront visiting the aquarium, the shops and the old pirate ship anchored in the harbor as a tourist attraction. You board the ship and step down into the cramped sleeping quarters where the pirates once bunked. Suddenly, on a shelf above one of the hammocks, you notice a small sea chest carved out of dark, oily wood. You look to see if anyone is watching, then pick up the chest. It is locked, so you set it down, but as you do, one of the legs falls off. You pick up the leg to insert it back into place, and a tiny tube of paper drops out. You quickly push the leg under the sea chest, put the paper tube in your pocket and leave.

At home in your room, you unroll the paper and find a sketch of the pirate ship, with an "X" drawn near the bottom of the ship, below the water line and directly beneath the ship's steering deck. You are sure it is a treasure map, and you will have to investigate or go crazy by noon tomorrow. You tell your friend Jordan, who doesn't believe you but who agrees to go along anyway.

It is a moonless midnight. An almost-tropical breeze wafts off the ocean. You slip into the water and swim under the dock, where the pirate ship is tied. No guards are in sight. You and Jordan steal aboard the ship and make your way to the sleeping quarters where you found the map. As you step into the darkness, a deep, mournful voice calls out, "Why have you come?" You freeze in terror as Jordan turns and races back up onto the deck . . .

Finish the story. What happened that night? Whose voice was it? How did you get out alive? What happened to Jordan? To the treasure? To the map?

_____

_____

_____

_____

_____

_____

_____

_____

_____

_____

_____

_____

Name _____

Waiting for Pop to Drop

Think of the precious seconds we all waste standing around waiting for machines to perform. We wait for microwave ovens to beep, for copy machines to spit out their papers, for irons to heat up, for computers to print and for clothes dryers to buzz. In a year's time, a person could easily consume 360 minutes, or six hours, just staring at the magnets on the refrigerator while soup heats up for 60 seconds in the microwave.

Six hours waiting in front of a microwave oven!

On the lines below, tell about the machines you have waited for in the past 12 months, and estimate the number of hours in a year that you wasted. Then write a list of things you could have done with the hours you frittered away while waiting.

_____

_____

_____

_____

_____

_____

_____

_____

_____

_____

_____

_____

_____

_____

_____

_____

_____

_____

_____

_____

Comeback Comments

Have you ever gone to buy an item of clothing, only to have the clerk look at you and say, "Are you sure this is your size?" Have you ever just about made it to the front door of your house dressed for an outing with friends when your mother or father says, "Are you wearing *those* pants again?" Do you recall ever getting pinched on the cheek by a large, perfumed aunt or a bald uncle who bent over you and said, "Don't you look just like your mother?"

Would you like to have replied with an annoying comment of your own — but you couldn't because you are too nice and polite? Well, here's your chance. Below are irritating comments made by a variety of persons. On the lines below each comment, write a *comeback comment* that puts the speaker in his or her place. You may never be able to say these things in public in the real world, but have fun with them on paper now.

1. Camp counselor: "Are we having fun in our crafts time with Ms. Mirkle?"

   _____

   _____

2. Friend: "What did you do to your hair?"

   _____

   _____

3. Parent: "Did you think I wouldn't find out?"

   _____

   _____

4. Hair stylist: "Does your mother (or father) know you're having this done?"

   _____

   _____

5. Teacher: "Do I have to call your parents?"

   _____

   _____

Flying High

Have you ever watched stunt pilots at work? They run a specially-built, short-winged plane straight up into the sky, then drop like a stone, pull out of the fall and almost scrape the earth with the belly of the plane as they swoop past the crowd and roar off into the clouds.

What if other professions had certain people who considered themselves daredevils? How would a "stunt plumber" conduct himself or herself, if given the chance to perform? How about a stunt dentist? A stunt librarian?

Write a brief description of the behavior of at least three of the daredevils below. Be creative. Be wild. Take risks with that dangerous pen of yours.

- a stunt plumber
- a stunt mail carrier
- a stunt baker
- a stunt librarian
- a stunt dentist

- a stunt bus driver
- a stunt photographer
- a stunt florist
- a stunt band director
- a stunt farmer

_____

_____

_____

_____

_____

_____

_____

_____

_____

_____

_____

_____

_____

_____

_____

_____

Car Salesman Boogie

Few things are more interesting to watch than a grown man selling cars on television. He might be dressed in a clown suit, or he might be wearing a cowboy hat and riding a horse. He might be dressed for tennis, waving a tennis racket and yelling, "This is not a racket, folks! This is Honest Billy Bob Wilson telling you to get down here today! Now is the time to buy! We'll get you on the road in the car of your choice for no money at all! If you can beat our deals we'll give you the car — NO, we'll give you the entire dealership! There's no better time to buy from Honest Billy Bob Wilson. I'll treat you right and serve you hot dogs while you wait. There are balloons for the kids and Pepto-Bismol for Grandma! Don't wait! The car or truck of your dreams is here with your name on it! That's the truth, or I'm not Honest Billy Bob saying make a deal TODAY!"

What if other professions used the same techniques to do business? Choose one of the characters listed below (or come up with one of your own), and write a wild and crazy car-salesman-type advertisement that is sure to stir people out of their easy chairs to come down and buy, buy, buy! (You may want to use a couple of sentences to describe the physical setting and the costume that your salesperson is wearing before you actually go into the sales pitch.)

> dentist • computer salesperson • minister/priest/rabbi • hair stylist •
> chiropractor • teacher • police officer • fire fighter • business owner •
> jeweler • bus driver • bank teller • arcade owner • lifeguard • mechanic •
> attorney • fortuneteller • animal trainer • lawn care specialist •
> baby sitter • sanitation worker • truck driver • umpire • cartoonist •

_____

_____

_____

_____

_____

_____

_____

_____

Name _____

Unlucky You

You are the unluckiest person in the world. Two summers ago you won a case of dog food on a call-in radio show, but you had a pet bird at the time. Last year you broke your foot the day before soccer camp. Last month you borrowed the neighbor's riding lawn mower and drove into the back of his new car. It has been a tough life.

Now you have been selected to appear on a game show called "A Walk on the Wet Side." You are sitting backstage getting powder daubed on your shiny forehead and feeling nervous. Suddenly the door opens. It's Amber Wholesome, who directs guests on stage and helps them off when their segment is over. "We're ready for you now," she says. You take one last look in the mirror at a very pale you, then follow Amber down the hallway into the bright lights.

You make television history, becoming part of the worst "A Walk on the Wet Side" episode ever filmed. What happened? (How is the game played? What was expected of you? What went wrong?) Finish the story of the unluckiest day of your unlucky life.

_____

_____

_____

_____

_____

_____

_____

_____

_____

_____

_____

_____

_____

_____

_____

_____

_____

Speak Up!

You are the world's finest orator. You have given speeches at important gatherings all over the world. Last year you were in Chicago as the keynote speaker for the members of the Video Arcade Token Designers Association. Six months ago you went to Tokyo to deliver a speech to the National Convention of Japanese Comedians.

There are seven groups that want you for their keynote speaker on the first Saturday of next month. All are willing to pay your standard $50,000 fee, but you can speak to only one group, of course. Choose the group that will be lucky enough to have you, and write the introduction to your speech in the space provided.

- National Convention of People Who Claim They Have Seen Elvis Appear as a Clerk in Wal-Mart

- National Convention of People Who Have Eaten Microwaved Squid and Lived to Tell About It

- International Convention of People with Feet that Are the Same Size as Cinderella's

- National Gathering of People Rejected as Game Show Participants

- International Convention of the Society of Anchovy Trainers

- National Convention of Parents Whose Children Will One Day Be President

- National Convention of People Who Claim to Have Driven Their Mini-Vans to Other Planets

Reality, Please

There is often a great gap between what really happens in our lives, and what is *supposed* to happen. People say, "Enjoy your school days; they are the best days of your life!" But to many young people, school seems to plod on forever, and the days are filled with work, rules and strange noon meals. The reality, to some people, is that school just isn't all it's cracked up to be.

Life is like that. Reality is often different than what we might wish.

Below are listed some statements that we all hear in real life. Sometimes the statements are true, but sometimes they are not. After each statement, describe what *really* happens when reality is different than anticipated.

1. A statement about Thanksgiving Day: "Don't worry. The leftovers will be gone by Tuesday."
   The reality:

2. A statement about the first day of preschool: "Don't worry, honey. School will be fun."
   The reality:

3. A statement about a blind date: "Hey. Be cool. This guy (girl) is perfect!"
   The reality:

4. A statement from the dentist: "Relax. You won't feel a thing."
   The reality:

5. A statement from Mom to you: "You're going to love having a baby sister (brother)!"
   The reality:

6. A statement from Dad to you: "Try some of the casserole. It's delicious!"
   The reality:

A Fairly Weird Fairy Tale

Do you remember the fairy tales of childhood — *Rumpelstiltskin, Little Red Riding Hood, Goldilocks and the Three Bears, Jack and the Beanstalk, The Three Little Pigs, Sleeping Beauty, Cinderella, Snow White* and *Hansel and Gretel?* Have some fun making up a new fairy tale of your own, based on at least FIVE of the characters from the tales listed above. Write all five into the same story.

Ideas: How would Goldilocks feel if the Three Little Pigs came home instead of the Three Bears? What if Hansel and Gretel climbed the beanstalk, then slipped and fell on top of Little Red Riding Hood? What would Sleeping Beauty say if she were kissed by Rumpelstiltskin and woke up at Cinderella's house, where the wicked stepsisters were getting ready to kidnap the seven dwarfs and take them to Grandma's house? You can see that all this could be a little confusing, and a lot of fun, if you let your imagination run wild for a while. In the space below, write a fairy tale that makes the original tales look tame and boring.

_____

_____

_____

_____

_____

_____

_____

_____

_____

_____

_____

_____

_____

_____

_____

_____

Tabloid Times

Did you know that a parrot in Pittsburgh gave birth to twin puppies that resemble goldfish? Did you know that on moonless nights, aliens from Saturn meet at shopping malls to buy rap albums and eat bagels?

If you think these stories are a little weird, you are right. But every day, newspapers called *tabloids* print stories far more bizarre than either of these. No matter how unbelievable the tales, people continue to buy tabloids in greater and greater numbers.

Pretend you are a reporter for a tabloid paper called *The Sneak*. You have been given the assignment to cover the national scene from New York to Los Angeles for a period of one week. Write either a sports story, a news item, a personal interview, a gossip column, an advice column or a health tip — but write it in unique, shocking tabloid style.

Be creative. Be wild. Try to come up with a bizarre, alarming title to hook your readers. Most important, remember to make your article weird!

(You might actually type your article, combine it with others from your class and create a complete tabloid. Who knows — you might become real competition for the *National Enquirer!*)

_____

_____

_____

_____

_____

_____

_____

_____

_____

_____

_____

_____

_____

_____

_____

_____

_____

Revenge of the Critic

You tried writing screenplays, but that didn't work out. You tried acting, but the director said "Cut!" and he meant you. You tried producing an underwater situation comedy, but no TV stations would show it.

Now you are in Hackensack, New Jersey, working as a television critic. You watch six to ten television shows each week, writing reviews for several different magazines and newspapers around the country. One night you are watching a show called "Fetch," about a dog who trains people to do stupid tricks. Suddenly, something snaps. You have had it.

You are furious that shows like this make it on television, while all of your wonderful work was never even given a chance. The entire industry has ignored you, especially producer Irvine LaFocus, who runs the biggest production company in Hollywood, and who treated you like a ticket stub the first time you met him. You decide to write a review of one of his shows, and this time you are going to say how you *really* feel about the show.

On the lines below, write the title of the show you are going to review. Then follow with the most scathing, hilarious, ridiculous, scandalous review you have ever written. The show you write about might be a soap opera, a comedy, a drama, a sitcom, a cartoon, a game show or anything at all that you have wished could be wiped off the airwaves with the flick of a fly swatter.

_____

_____

_____

_____

_____

_____

_____

_____

_____

_____

_____

_____

Howling for Justice

You are a lawyer defending a cat in a capital murder case. Two poodles turned up as dead as dog dishes on Halloween night, and your client, Elaine Calico, was caught at the scene sitting on the rim of the dumpster that held the bodies.

You are in the courtroom of Judge Bellows, an Irish wolfhound who takes no nonsense from upstart young beagles like yourself. The jury, unfortunately, is all dogs — two dalmations, a dachshund, two cocker spaniels, two labrador retrievers, three beagles, and two poodles. The poodles are pink and freshly barbered, so they will be tough to convince; the victims were pink and freshly barbered, too.

Elaine has told you of her past, which is shady, but you believe in her innocence. On the night of the murder, she was strolling down the alley at 64th and Vine when she smelled the aroma of spoiled barbecued ribs. She followed her nose to the dumpster behind the Silly Kittens Restaurant, where she often found late night snacks for her and her 18 kittens. When she jumped to the rim of the dumpster she saw the two lifeless poodles. She was about to run for a phone when two squad cars full of German shepherds pulled up and arrested her for first pedigree murder.

Tell how you will defend Elaine Calico. Will you claim feline insanity and go for a lesser sentence? Will you cross examine the greyhound couple who say they saw Elaine entering the alley just ahead of the poodles, at about 2 AM? Will you put Elaine on the stand? How are you going to convince 12 angry dogs to let your client go free? Be wise. Be careful. Don't throw away your career for a purrrty face.

_____

_____

_____

_____

_____

_____

_____

_____

_____

_____

_____

Absolutely Perfect

Name _____

Rory Stevenson woke to the sounds and smells of a summer morning: birds chirping in the apple tree outside the window, the hum of a street-paving machine with its licorice smells of hot tar and gravel, the rumble of the Greyhound bus pulling away from Hanson's General Store two blocks over. It was the start of another perfect day in Greentown — too perfect, really. Rory had been bothered by the town's perfection ever since the Stevenson family had moved there a year and a half ago. Nothing ever seemed to go wrong. The right amount of snow fell in winter. The perfect amount of sun warmed the crystal lakes in summer. Blueberries hung ripe and ready along the narrow country roads outside of town in August. It was all starting to get to Rory, *really* get to him.

One day he found himself frowning at a shiny town statue of Roger Greenwood. Then he looked at the town fountain, at the perfectly red geraniums in the city hall window boxes and at the perfectly mowed lawns as far as he could see. He decided he had to act. He decided to set to work that very night. He would add some spice to Greentown. He would make people sit up and take notice. He would make the town, for at least one day, less irritatingly perfect than it had always been — and without doing any damage.

Describe Rory's actions. How does the touch of a teenager make the town of Greentown more interesting?

_____

_____

_____

_____

_____

_____

_____

_____

_____

_____

_____

_____

_____